IMAGES
of England

WIDNES
The Second Selection

Old and new lighthouses at Hale Point, c. 1910. At this point the Mersey is three miles across, and very shallow. At low tide a huge sand bank appears stretching from Hale to Weston, the route of the old ford. Many ships have foundered off Hale and Oglet over the years. The first lighthouse was erected in 1836 and the light-keeper's house was converted from a bathing house previously used by the Blackburne family. Unfortunately this lighthouse did not reduce the number of wrecks and by 1906 it was decided to build a larger one. When finished the new house had a lamp that was 70 feet above sea level and could be seen 40 miles away. During 1958 it ceased to operate following the reduction in traffic on the river and also because buoys were by then being used to mark the channels.

IMAGES *of England*

WIDNES
THE SECOND SELECTION

Compiled by
Stan Hall and the Widnes Historical Society

TEMPUS

First published 2001
Copyright © Stan Hall and the Widnes Historical Society, 2001

Tempus Publishing Limited
The Mill, Brimscombe Port,
Stroud, Gloucestershire, GL5 2QG

ISBN 0 7524 2253 7

Typesetting and origination by
Tempus Publishing Limited
Printed in Great Britain by
Midway Colour Print, Wiltshire

Half of St Mary's parish seen from the top of the Widnes tower of the Transporter bridge in 1937 showing Widnes Dock, Mersey Road, West Bank School, Boltons and various other recognisable places of interest (for the view looking the other way see p 65).

Contents

Foreword 6

Introduction 7

Acknowledgements 8

1. Bridging the Mersey 9

2. Industry 21

3. Transport 35

4. Schools and Sports 47

5. Church and Chapel 55

6. Farnworth 69

7. Hale and Hale Hall 79

8. Rainhill 89

9. Cronton 103

10 People and Places 109

Foreword

It is a privilege to be invited to write the foreword to this second book of photographs on Widnes and its neighbourhood, collected and described by Mr S. Hall, a member of the Widnes Historical Society. Mr and Mrs Hall and the society collaborated in producing the first book of Widnes photographs which was published in 1995 and was an immediate success.

It is highly appropriate that this second publication is to be available in 2001, the 50th anniversary of the Widnes Historical Society's foundation in April 1951. Mr Hall is a Widnesian whose great-uncle, W. Hall, was a local photographer and publisher of picture postcards, many of Widnes, at the beginning of the twentieth century. He is in an almost unique position to choose and describe the pictures in this book. He has done this with masterly skill.

Of all the sources of local history, I believe illustrations, and in particular photographs, are the most rewarding to study for facts and clues about the past. In this book much social history of the Widnes area is recorded. The publication will appeal not only to Widnesians but to local historians everywhere.

I wish this publication every success!

J.A.J. Walker,
President
The Widnes Historical Society

Introduction

This second volume of Widnes in *The Archive Photographs Series* builds on the themes used in our first collection. The bridges over the Mersey at Widnes form some of the most enduring images of the town and fascinate local people who remember, in particular, the girders, cables, rivets and the nuts and bolts of the great Transporter bridge. Express trains and heavy freights still thunder over the railway bridge (the oldest of them all), though the closure of the footpath means that the thrill of the noise and vibration can now only be experienced from a distance. The great arch of the road bridge, more impressive now that it is floodlit at night, dominates the scene for miles away, though even with its new network of access roads it is barely adequate for the volume of traffic now using it and soon another bridge will have to be built to relieve the pressure on it, adding another chapter to the history of river crossings at Runcorn Gap.

The heavy chemical industry that has dominated this area for so long is now all but a memory in Widnes, some plants struggle on, but most have gone, taking jobs and money with them. It is strange to think that there is now no ICI presence in Widnes, the few plants that remain are no longer part of ICI, having been sold off to other companies.

Farmland, and indeed virtually any green space in the town, is fast disappearing under new housing developments. No land is available for improving the town centre without tearing down existing property, old and new. The old market has gone, and soon Simm's Cross School will follow, to be replaced by a new superstore and attendant car parks.

We have included in this book photographs of some of the areas of Widnes which at one time had strong ties to the township; Rainhill, Cronton (a part of the old Chapelry of Farnworth) and Hale (all of which are now part of the Deanery of Widnes) which lost their link with Widnes when local government boundaries were changed in 1974.

We have also included references to some of the personalities from the past who were important in the creation of the town and its industries. The pictures in this selection are a blend of the very old and not so old, and we have tried to keep a cut-off date around 1960 although there are a few more recent ones included when we felt that what they illustrate is important.

We hope you will enjoy this second walk through Widnes' past.

Stan Hall
Widnes
May 2001

Widnes West Bank Dock, c. 1920.

Acknowledgements

The photographs in this collection were assembled mainly with the help of members and friends of the Widnes Historical Society and I extend the Society's grateful thanks to:
Mr George Breeden, Mr Albert Stubbs, Mr G. Howarth, Mr and Mrs B. Clews, Mr G. Platt, Mr and Mrs A. Tickle, Mr and Mrs T. Jones, Mr E. Lyn, Mrs E. Lyn, Mrs A. Atherton, Mr W. Follows, Mrs V. Pickstock and Mrs J. Wallace.

Original glass plate negatives have been used to produce some of the prints and it must be remembered that some of these are now over one hundred years old.

Special thanks go to Mr J.A.J. Walker for his excellent reference work on Farnworth church and for use of his photographic archives.

Thanks to Mr D. Hall for his help with photographic prints and Mr P. Hall for typing and research. Finally I give my thanks to St Ambrose church for access to their Millenium Record.

One
Bridging the Mersey

An artist's impression of the Mersey Ferry loading on the Runcorn side in the days before the Manchester Ship Canal was built. Both the bathhouse and the hotel can be seen.

A very choppy river. An early paddle steamer is being used as a tug. Across the river Halton Castle, a windmill, a church and signs of early industry can all be seen. The painting is believed to be from around 1890.

Another painting depicts the rural-looking banks of the Mersey on the Runcorn side before the canal and the harbour were built. Bathers form a circle and play in the water while others sit on the edge and watch around 1890.

This view dates from after the canal was finished and the railway bridge was completed. Construction is under way for the Transporter bridge on the Runcorn side, 1904.

A view of the Transporter from the top looking through the curving cables and girder trellis which had such a fascination for so many Widnes people. The bridge spanned both the river and the Ship Canal, clearly visible in this photograph, with a span of around 1,000 ft.

11

Looking down onto Mersey Road from one of the Transporter towers. Buses had to back round to the queue at the Mersey Hotel and then head up the road into Widnes. This picture, taken probably in the 1930s, contains lots of interesting detail of this area and deserves a close look!

The Transporter bridge was opened by Sir John Brummer MP on 29 May 1905. Only four bridges of this kind, carrying road vehicles on a suspended platform, were built in Britain. The others were built at Middlesborough across the Tees in 1911, at Warrington, across the Mersey, linking two parts of a chemical firm, in 1916 and at Newport (Monmouthshire) across the river Usk, in 1906.

A busy dockside scene on St Helens Canal. Unloading and loading takes place outside Gossages Soap Works at Spike Island, *c.* 1897.

13

Many postcards like this one were offered for sale, proudly detailing the bridge's measurements and capabilities.

An excellent aerial view of cars being transported over the river. Judging by the vehicles on the platform this photograph was probably taken inz the mid-1930s.

Another fascinating view of Transporter in action, this time from the Widnes side, heading for Runcorn. Notice that the bicycles were allowed on last and would therefore be off last too! This scene was probably recorded on the same day as the previous one.

Another view of the bridge in action with a long queue of traffic waiting on the Widnes side, 1930s.

Well-maintained and strong though the bridge was, a ripple still appeared in the girders as the trolley, from which the car was suspended, travelled along. Two huge electric motors powered a winch that drew the platform along on thick cables. The bridge finally became redundant in 1961 when the adjacent arch bridge was opened.

The West Bank Viaduct with the ICI power station up and working. A Coronation class steam locomotive leads a train over the bridge heading for Liverpool. These locomotives were only introduced in 1937 and so the picture is probably from the late 1930s.

Construction of the new road bridge has started and the Transporter is still in use, c. 1959. Taken from the Runcorn side this photograph shows the girders of the new arch on the Widnes side. The heavy steel to the right is part of the base of the east supporting tower of the Transporter.

A start is made on the new bridge on the Runcorn side. The old ticket office and waiting-room can be seen on the right.

18

The skew arch was built to span the existing railway line to the West Bank Dock. This meant that the line could stay as it was without the need for any alteration and the Bridge line could still follow its planned curve.

This lock gave access to and from the Widnes Dock and the river at high tide.

One of W. Hall's excellent photographs of the Transporter soon after its opening. The celebratory flags are still in place.

Two
Industry

Casting copper ingots in a dark and dismal shed at Thomas Bolton's Mersey Copper Works (Dolphin Works), c. 1940. The firm was established in 1783.

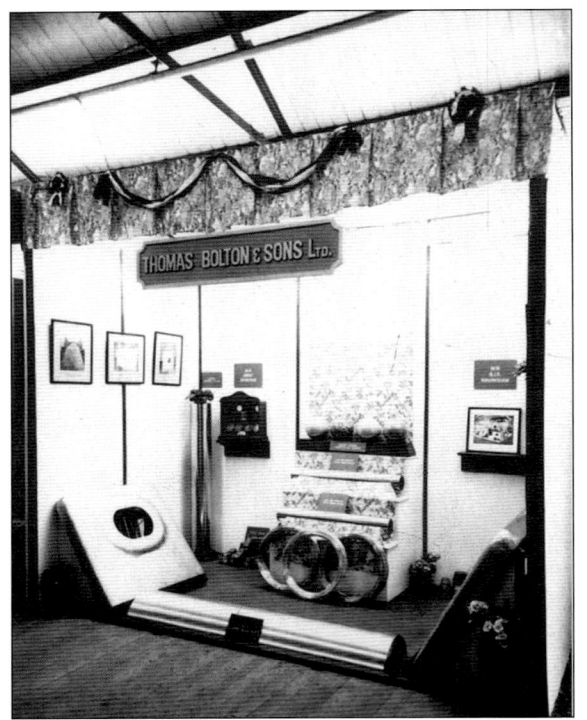

Thomas Bolton and Sons erected trade stands at many exhibitions throughout the country. To the left of centre on a wall rack there is a display of medals won at the Great Exhibition in 1851. Copper floats top the central, stepped display. Below this are blocks of copper sulphate and rolls of copper tubing. To the left is a furnace door and at the front are copper alloy covers.

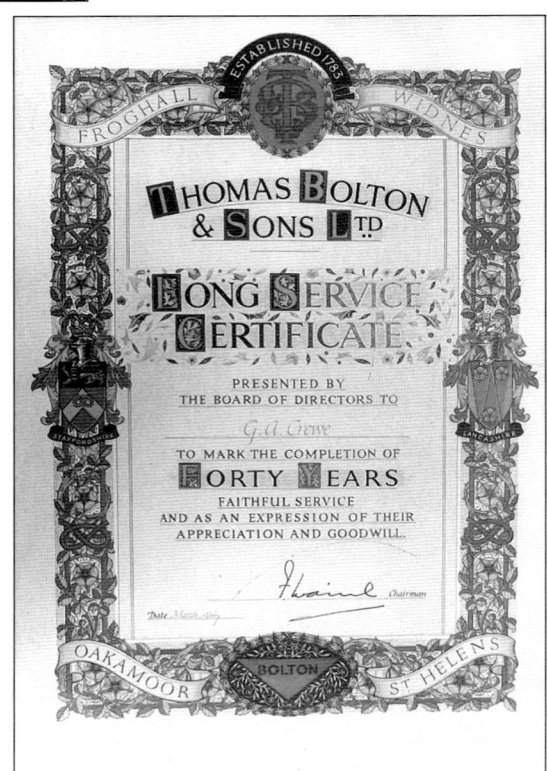

The long service certificate presented to G.A. Crewe after forty years working for Thomas Bolton & Sons.

22

A well stacked truck, 1920s. This vehicle, owned by the Calder and Mersey Extract Company Ltd, is loaded up with seventy-two barrels of tanning extract ready for departure from their Ditton Brook wharfage site.

During the 1950s and '60s Foxall's Engineering of Liverpool had contracts with ICI to test and repair lifting equipment. Here the firm of Pilkington-Sullivan load some suspect gear onto a Foxall's truck.

23

Penketh Tannery to the east of Widnes produced leather for the clothing and footwear industries for many years. When it closed down in the 1950s Polycell used part of the building to make tiles but this soon closed down too.

The firm of J.W. Towers made laboratory and specialist glassware. Now only the stone laid to commemorate their Diamond Jubilee in 1942 survives. Their speciality was calibrated glassware for laboratories all over the world. During the war years many local women were employed at home by Towers to make glass detonators. They were provided with heat proof work tops, electric blowers for power burners, gauges and files and made small glass bulbs, three-sixteenths of an inch in diameter with a stem one-quarter of an inch long which were filled with an acid and used to detonate bombs. Some women made 3,000 per week!

Widnes Foundry made, among other items, tubular fencing rails and girders used in many coastal piers around the country, all clearly marked Widnes Foundry. Some castings and fabrications were so long they had to be manouevred on special bogeys with individual motors and steering. This, and the next two photographs, show such a bogey in use to move an enormous casting out of the foundry in the late 1960s.

The bogey is seen here being used to make a tight turn.

The long load is now out of the foundry and ready for its journey, hauled by a heavy duty Pickford's truck.

A steam wagon belonging to Richard Allen is dwarfed by its huge cargo, a plated hopper, as it moves off, sometime in the early part of the last century.

Another Pickford's truck hauls a casting out of the Widnes Foundry, this time in the early 1950s. In the casting process vessels had a lining of brick and sand which became fused together with the heat. Women were often employed to knock this hot mixture out. It was a dirty, hot, gritty and dusty job.

William Gossage with some of his workers.

Fifty years ago a new pipeline to Liverpool was laid from North Wales bringing much needed water to the expanding city. This and the following sequence of photographs show some of this work going on and some of the men who were involved as it made its way round Widnes.

Across from Runcorn the pipeline came, under the Manchester Ship Canal, the Mersey, Widnes Marsh, and The Sankey Navigation Canal which was dammed off and the muddy bottom trenched. The pipe was placed in it and the mud seal was replaced.

28

Waiting for a brew. Pipeline workers pose in front of Fiddler's Ferry power station which was still being constructed.

Work was hard so swinging over the trench provided a bit of light relief.

Pipeline work speeds up as the machinery arrives.

The sections are sealed as soon as they are put in, keeping the inside clean and free from contamination.

The remaining part of this chapter shows some of the pioneers of the local chemical industry. Widnesians often express interest in these early industrialists whose names live on in the locality but about whom little is known.

John Hutchinson (1825-1865) built the first factory of any importance in Widnes making alkali. In 1847 this was known as Hutchinson's No. 1. He was just twenty-two years old when he opened this first factory - what an achievement! His family came from the North East and his father served in the Navy under Nelson during the Napoleonic Wars. Profits and investments helped him to buy land in Widnes and soon he was a major land-owner. He used some of this land for more factories and some provided space for tips of chemical waste.

John McClellan (1810-1881). John McClellan concentrated on the production of borax and tartar salts in Widnes. Later in Lugsdale he made alkali and borax. He was much involved in municipal affairs, and became Chairman of the Board. Railwaymen recall him when they refer to a length of line near his Lugsdale works, as 'McClellan's Slip.'

William Gossage (1799-1877) was born in Lincolnshire and went to Chesterfield where he trained as an apothecary in his uncle's shop. In 1855 he moved to Widnes to set up as a soap-maker a trade in which he became very successful. He was the first Chairman of the Local Board.

James Muspratt (1793-1886) was the first to develop the Leblanc soda process on an industrial scale in this country. Most importantly he created a market for this synthetic alkali by overcoming the suspicion of the soap boilers who traditionally used barilla and kelp. His son Frederic carried on the family business at Woodend.

Henry Deacon (1822-1874) was a Londoner and a pupil of Michael Faraday who came to Widnes as Hutchinson's assistant in 1848. By 1853 he had set up his own works attempting to make soda by the ammonia process but was not successful. William Pilkington, his partner, left him, but Holbrook Gaskell supported Deacon financially who then went back to using the more reliable Leblanc process. He died from typhoid fever.

Holbrook Gaskell (1813-1909) was born in Liverpool and became a partner of Nasmyth, the inventor of the steam hammer and then joined Deacon in Widnes. The firm of Gaskell, Deacon and Company making alkalis prospered. On the formation of the United Alkali Company, Gaskell became a Vice-President and then President.

Dr Ferdinand Hurter (1844-1898) became a chemist at the Gaskell-Deacon works in 1867, working with Henry Deacon to develop what became known as the Deacon-Hurter chlorine process. For about half a century this was the principal method for making chlorine. In 1891 he founded the Central Laboratory of the United Alkali Company and was a leading authority on the production of chlorine with his friend, Vero Charles Driffield, Hurter laid the foundations of scientific photography in research carried out in Widnes from 1876-1898.

Three
Transport

Widnes Town Council were taken around Widnes in this steam driven wagon to see the decorations for King Edward VII's coronation in 1902. The vehicle was owned by Richard Allens and was one of the first Foden steam wagons to be produced.

A Richard Allen wagon takes on a load of wire at the Sankey Wire Works in Warrington in the early years of the last century. Richard Allen stands proudly by his vehicle.

Beckett Brothers took over and developed a haulage business in Halton View at the lower end of Ireland Street in the 1930s. This is one of their promotional photographs. This site is now occupied by houses.

The Becketts developed a Liverpool to the Potteries daily service operating from Widnes but eventually the business moved out of town. This photograph is from around 1950.

A bus conductor waits for the return run at the old Black Horse, 1910.

This splendid Tilling Stevens bus belonging to Widnes Corporation pauses for a photograph by the Transporter bridge in the 1920s. Mr and Mrs Pickstock of Widnes are on board. A notice on the bus window warns of imminent fare increases.!

One of the Penketh Tannery's own steam wagons, c. 1905.

Two of Rugby League's greats, Jack and Alec Higgins, with Jack's wagon in the 1930s. Alec leans and Jack is in the cab.

A hale and hearty group of farm workers with a steam traction engine which was probably used for driving the threshing machine, 1920s. In the group are, left to right: Joe Humphreys, Bernard Dunbar, Jim Woodward, Martin Muldoon, -?-.

All safely delivered! The driver from A.R.Sutton and Sons, Lea Green (notice his gaiters), poses for a picture after neatly piling up the folded coal sacks on the cart before heading home in around 1930.

Another large convoy of trucks from Edward Box of Liverpool waiting to leave the Widnes Foundry, c. 1946.

One of a fleet of new thirty-eight seater Bedford Duple Vega coaches ordered in 1955 by Mr H. Scragg for use by his company. Mr Scragg is quoted as saying that, 'They represent craftmanship of a high order.'

The Regal Garage in Albert Road was the base for Clayton's Funeral Services. In 1946 Sexton and Scragg (Widnes) Ltd took over the premises as a coach station, running many trips and tours in and around Britain, between April and October each year.

45

Suttons have been in long distance heavy haulage for many years and currently work from Gorsey Lane, Widnes. This Sutton's ERF Light Diesel lorry, which ran between Liverpool and London, was photographed around 1980. The driver is Edward Foden.

Four
Schools and Sport

Warrington Road school cricket team who won the Widnes schools' trophy 1955/56. Among the group are: Done, Williams, Cooney, Mitchell, Winstanley, D'Arcy, Woodward, Rigby, Goggin, Shard, Newton and Johnson.

Miss Cartwright, a former head of Warrington Road infants school, presents house trophies to A. Bailey and C. Ireland in 1955. Mr W. Ankers, head of Warrington Road juniors, and Miss E. Cropper, head of Warrington Road infants, look on.

This group of young athletes from Warrington Road school won the Combined Athletics trophy, c. 1950.

Practice day at the Wade Deacon school 1946/47. Practices usually took place on Wednesdays, if there wasn't a match on that day. Any outfit was worn, the proper kit being saved for the matches.

Wade Deacon school 1st XV 1949/50. The players and staff are, left to right, back row: Mr J. D. Jones (coach), Wilson, Jones, Young, Mr W.H. Bonney (headmaster), Hall, Anderson, Smith, Mr A. Salt. Middle row: Broadhurst, Riding, Leigh, Brown, Norman, Clare, Sutton. Front: Rogerson, Laws.

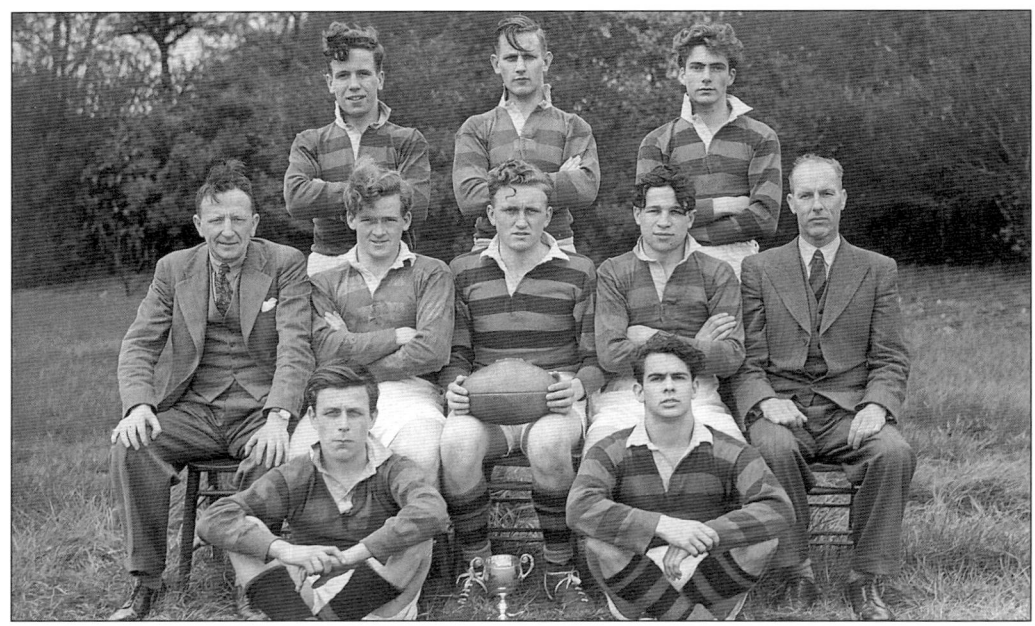

In 1949 Wade Deacon school won the Manchester Sevens. In 1950 the school was asked to enter two teams and the 1949 winners were entered as the 'A' Team. The 'B' Team, however, won. The 1950s winners are shown here. They are, left to right, back row: Broadhurst, Hall, Anderson. Middle row: Mr J.D. Jones, Smith, Young, Wilson, Mr W.H. Bonney. Front row: Parker, Rogerson.

Warrington Road junior boys' staff in the late 1950s. Two Malaysian students were at the school at the time, one stands at each end of the back row, the others are, left to right: S. Hall, F. Whyte (Ruby League winger), W. Ankers (headmaster) who had worked at Gossage's factory until its closure and then trained as a teacher, Jim McDonald. Front row: A.K. Wood, B. Ward, E. Connolly, N. Connor.

Widnes Secondary school football team had an excellent season 1911/12: won 12, drew 2, lost 1. The teacher on the left is Mr Dobson.

The very impressive upstairs corridor at Widnes Secondary school, next to the Widnes library.around 1900.

Farnworth Wesley Guild AFC 1910/1911. Mr Dobson (behind the wall) and Mr A. Salt, right have been recognised in this picture.

Everite baseball team 1950. Back row, left to right: R. Wallace, F. Smith, T. Rimmer, R. Standish, D. Meadon. Front row: J. Cain, E. Hartles, R. Cook, W. Burgess. There was a local league for baseball teams at this time.

Mr Dyer, and Mr H. Wallace were Gold Medal winners in the 1920s when this portrait was taken at the rear of 68, Farnworth Street, the Appleton Pool Club.

An afternoon garden party on the old vicarage lawn at St Ambrose with teas and clock golf for the ladies. Hargreaves House is now on this site.

Five
Church and Church Life

Rose Queen ceremonies were still very popular after the Second World War. Audrey Herriman is the Queen in this picture taken at St Ambrose church in 1955. Her retinue includes Beryl Smart, Maureen Halewood, Audrey Blackmore, Eileen Philips and Violet Griffiths.

John and Ethel Hillock on their wedding day in 1940. The Revd Bankes and Tom Jones are also in the group. John Hillock was a well known lay reader throughout the Liverpool Diocese.

Miss Margaret Beckett is the St Ambrose Rose Queen in this photograph taken in 1959. The gentleman in the striped blazer is the Revd Sydney Goddard, who undertook the organisation of the roof repairs and the eradication of dry rot discovered in the church. Mr F. Tuson carried out the repairs. Revd Goddard became very well known in his next ministry when he set up World Friendship House in Liverpool to help students from overseas.

Once a month the Sunday school at St Ambrose held an afternoon service which the mums and dads also attended. In this photograph, taken in the 1950s, the children are seen leaving the church. The little ones have already left, the juniors are on their way, soon to be followed by the seniors. We are able to name two sets of twins in this picture, the Yates' and the Evans', a Stead and another Yates, two Williams, a Ramsey, and a Dunne, the Linakers, a Lever, a Kirchin, the Puckeys, a Blower, an Oldham and the vicar's wife, Mrs Hoyle, with their first child.

Jubilee picture card for the Girls' Friendly Society produced in 1925. This society had been set up to help young women who had gone into service and who did not live near their homes. The Society was founded in 1875 by Mary Townsend and is an organisation that has moved and changed with the times continuing to adapt and work with commitment and faith.

St Ambrose church had a roof of small red tiles which were constantly breaking and so in the late 1950s they were replaced with larger, Everite tiles. This photograph shows the earlier roof.

This photograph sent from Kiel in Germany bears the message, 'To my dearest friends with best wishes, Werner. Christmas 1948 .' Werner Untiedt had been the interpreter for the German Prisoners of War at a service held on 3 May 1947 at the South Lane Hostel. St Ambrose church had been used by the Prisoners of War for Sunday afternoon services during the war.

58

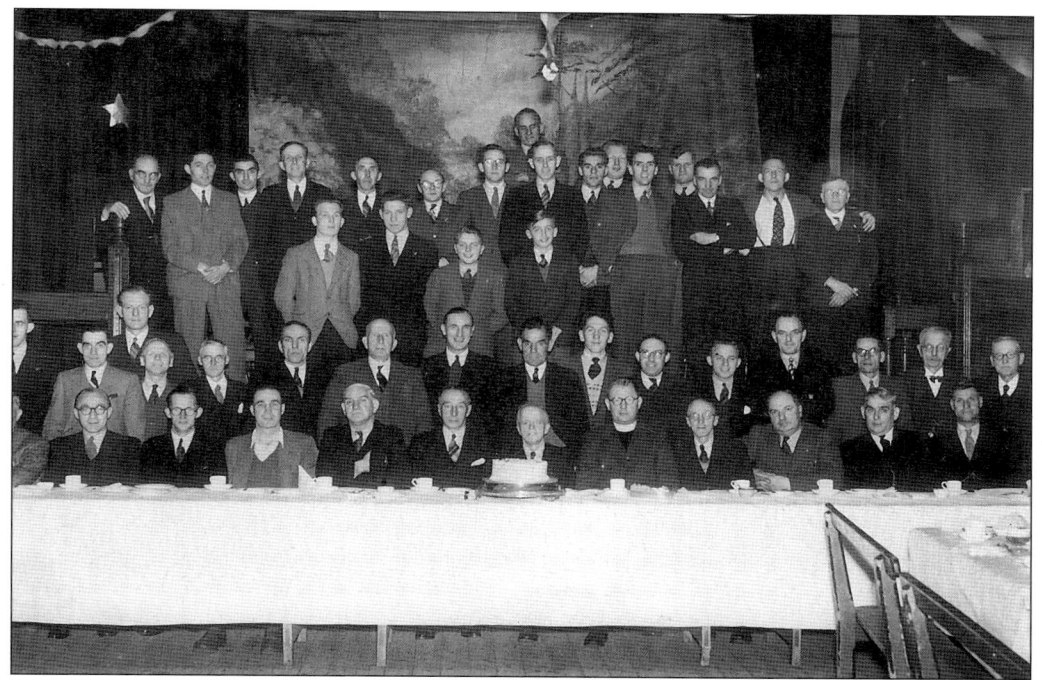

A 'Men and Boys Dinner' at Hartland Methodists in 1947. The Minister is Revd Davies and Lawrence Atherton is somewhere in the group.

This old postcard photograph shows the lovely reredos and sanctuary at St Pauls church in the old Town Hall Square.

Derby Road Methodists pose for a commemorative group photograph after completing an afternoon walk over Pex Hill in the early 1900s.

A group photographed at a garden party at Farnworth Methodist church in the late 1940s. Present (adults) were, left to right, Mr Odgers, Revd W.H. Stevens, Mrs Florence Richards (née Davies), Mrs Phyllis Breeden (née Davies and Florence's twin), -?-, -?-.

At the start of the Second World War, Mr and Mrs R. Earle were married at Hough Green church. The small gentleman with the moustache is the bride's father Mr G. Hunt.

The interior of the Victoria Road Wesleyan chapel in 1920, now the Queen's Hall. The magnificent organ was removed from here and relocated in the Wesley at the bottom of Peel House Lane, which had to be enlarged to make room for it. The Wesley was later demolished but the organ was saved and sold. That site is now occupied by the United Reform church.

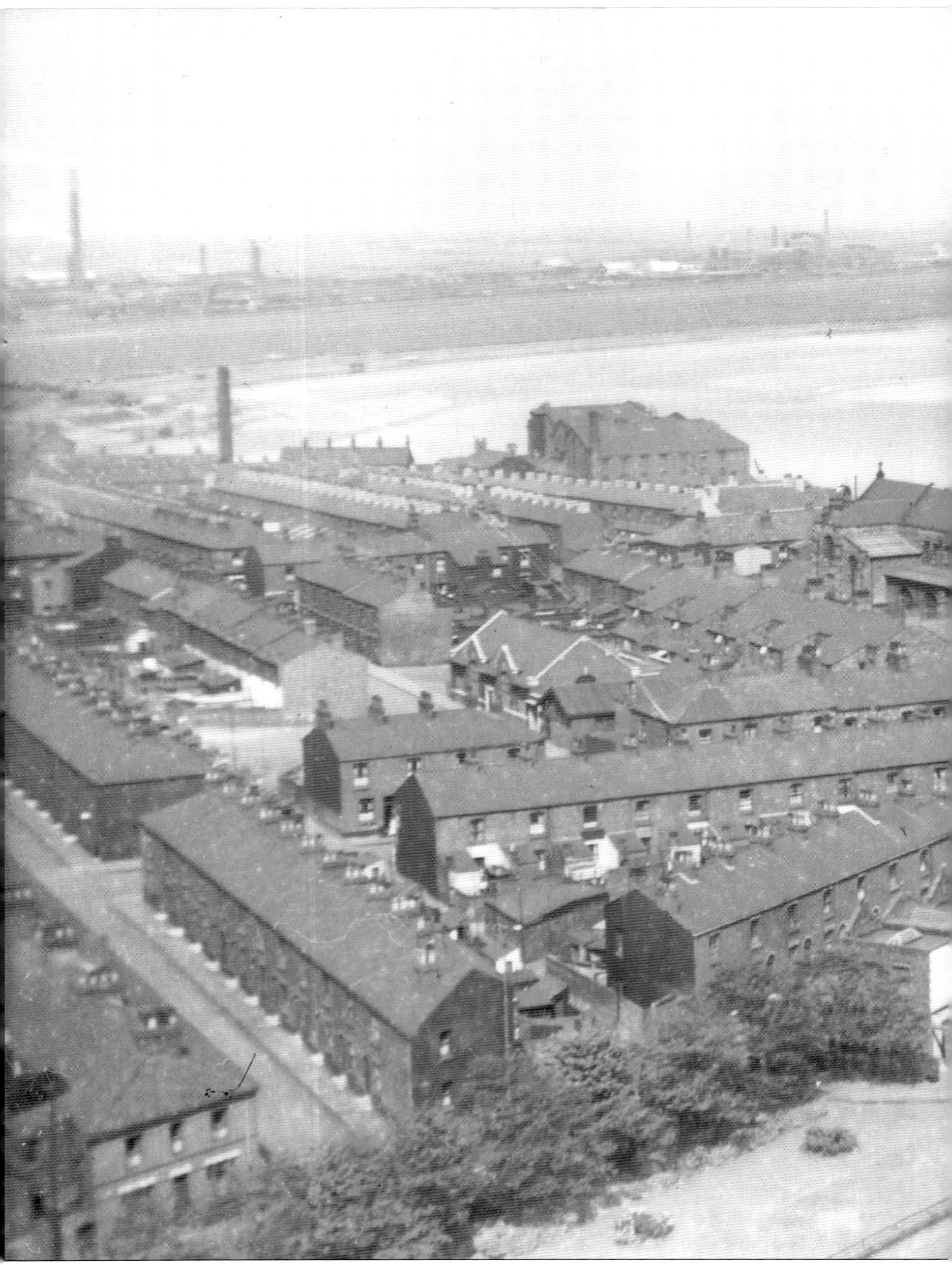

also the enormous silt beds in the river to be seen at low tides. around 1937.

A striking view of the tower at the new St Mary's. Architects Austin and Paley of Lancaster supervised the building programme from design to completion. The inside length is 150 ft 6 in. and the tower's height is 100 ft. The seating capacity is 770.

In the new church the Late Decorative style is very evident and the flecked red stone is well defined. The Red Ruabon tiles make a striking roof.

The pulpit at the new St Mary's church. Darley Dale stone was used to build this unique circular pulpit whose green marble rail adds to the overall beauty. St Paul and St John are represented on the side.

The entrance to the Lady (Morning) Chapel seen down the south aisle of St Mary's church.

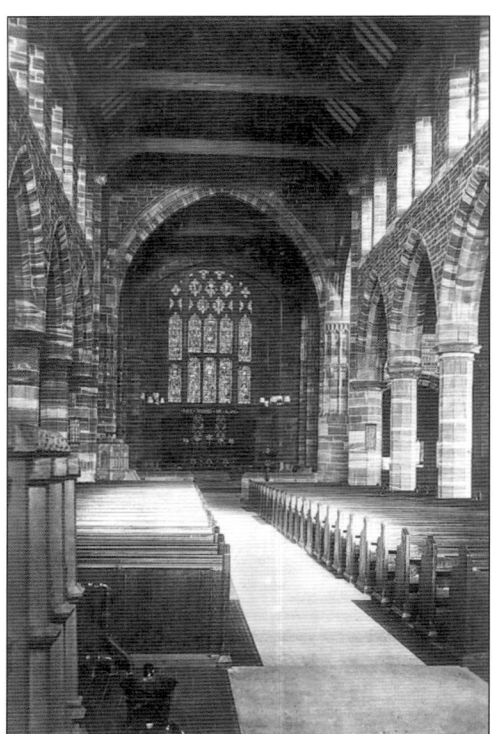

The centre aisle of St Mary's church. The flecked stone and the hexagonal pillars are shown to good advantage in this view.

A Sunday School Treat in 1923 stepping out with the band along Warrington Road. The boy right of centre in the front row of the band, wearing short trousers, is a young Mr A. Stubbs, who has played in several different bands over the years. He still lives in the area although he doesn't play any more.

Six
Farnworth

St Luke's church at the top of Farnworth Street. On the corner was the No. 17 branch of the Co-op which closed in 1906 when new Co-op shops opened in nearby Derby Road.

Farnworth church before its restoration in 1894. The south side of the church is to the left and the Bold Chapel on the right. This important old photograph has answered a question that had puzzled local people in recent years. Where were the old galleries located? There had clearly been galleries at the west end, for the organ loft and possibly the choir and in the south aisle but this picture also shows a gallery in the chancel. Off-set from the centre at the west end can be seen the tower arch, containing the organ, leading into the fourteenth-century tower. The bells in the tower were re-cast as a memorial after the last war. Notice the absence of a font and that there is a clock on the gallery front. Above the pillars on the north side are the hatchments of the families who were patrons of the church. Closer to the camera on the right is an ancient two-tiered pulpit. Tradition has it that the Gospel was read from the lower tier and explained from the upper. The churchwardens stood near here, facing the congregation, reputedly looking for signs of inattention, prodding members back into wakefulness with their wands! There is a small pedal organ on the right and in the corner a square stove with a chimney. This and its several companions were the sole means of heating the church. In the left foreground can be seen some of the enclosed pews, owned by some of the wealthier parishioners and reserved for their use. The magnificent light fittings seem to be without gas mantles yet the one in the pulpit has one.

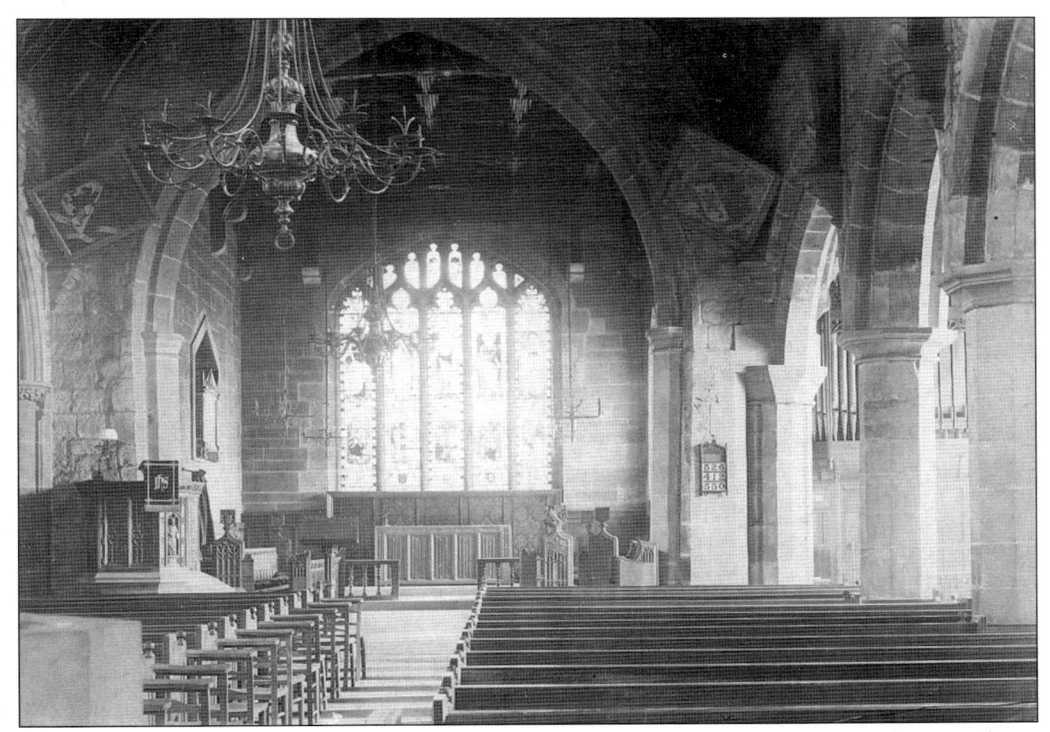

Farnworth church, this time seen from the east end and after the restoration. The pews have been rearranged, the galleries have gone, and the pulpit is new. The church is much lighter and brighter. The candelabra gas holders were later inverted to take electric lights.

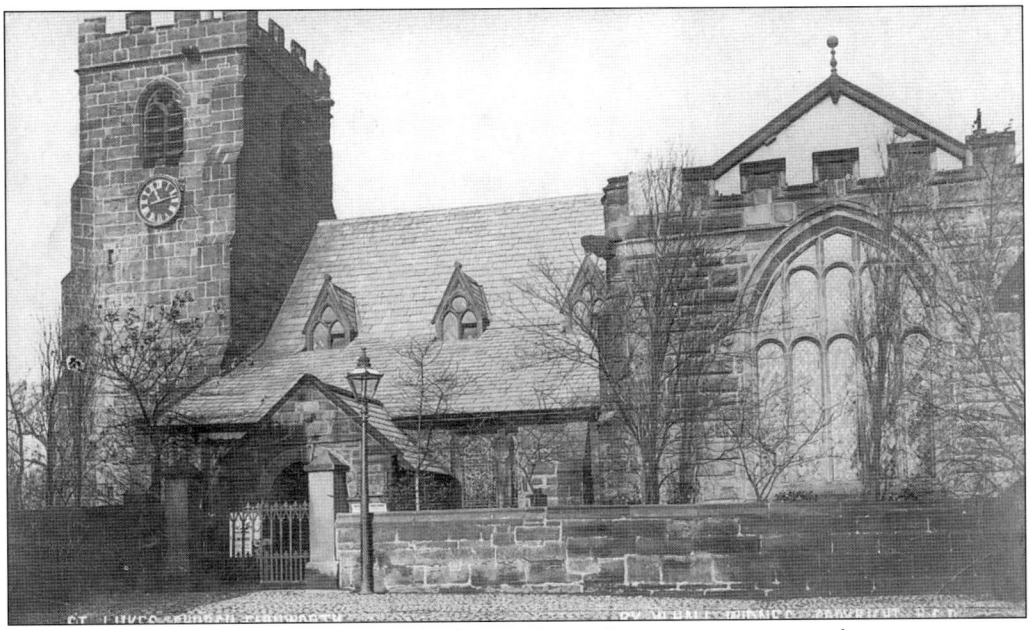

St Luke's church in about 1901. Very little has changed in its appearance today.

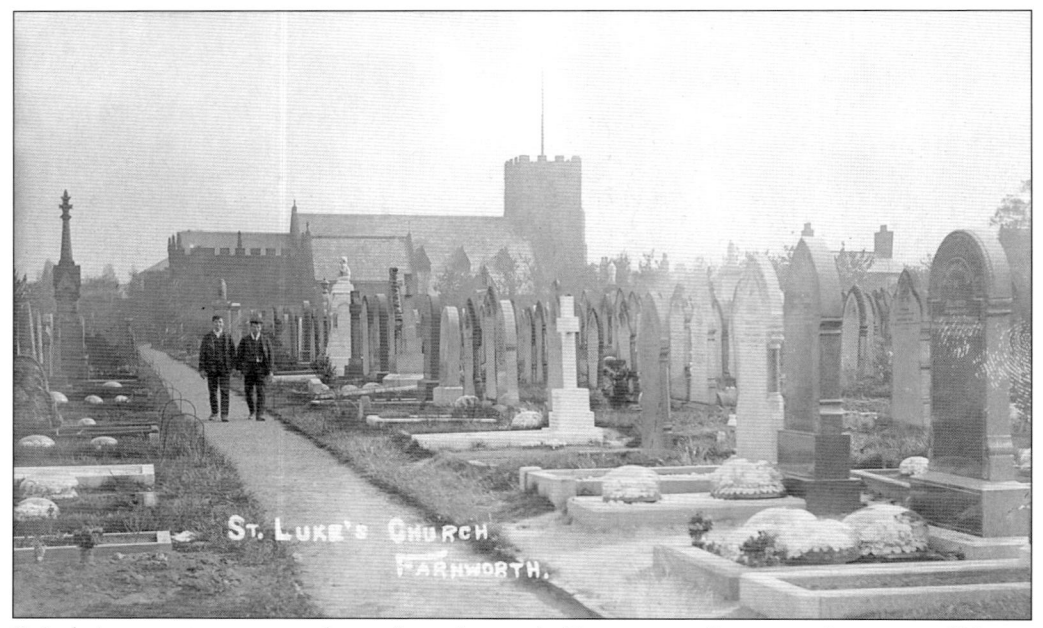

St Luke's extensive graveyard seen from the north. Two men walk near to the graves of Hurter and Driffield who were friends in life and did much research on photographic emulsions and produced standardized speeds for films (H and D numbers).

A memorial window in the south wall of St Luke's church dedicated to the memory of Emily Wright Williams, wife of the vicar, who died in April 1904. Notice that this photographic postcard was taken by W. Hall who gives his address at the bottom of the card and also asserts his copyright on the picture.

Farnworth Street, once called Church Street, c. 1930.

The Birchfield Road end of Coroner's Lane, c. 1910. This scene is still recognisable after all these years. The little lodge house is hidden just behind the foliage on the left of the lane.

Richard Bancroft 1544-1610 was born in September 1544 to John Bancroft, gentleman, and Mary his wife. He was well grounded in Latin at Farnworth Grammar School before being sent to Christ's College, Cambridge, being paid for by his uncle, Hugh Curwen, Bishop of Oxford. He gained his BA in 1566-67 and studied at Jesus College. He became Bishop of London and was present at the death of Queen Elizabeth I. He was elected Archbishop of Canterbury in 1604 and organised a new translation of the Bible, the first copy of which, in 1611, was presented to the King.

The family at Bold Hall has always had an association with Farnworth church and has its own chapel there. This scene in Bold Woods shows one of the ponds complete with swans.

Bold Woods with an Edwardian family reading and relaxing under the trees. Mr Hall, the photographer, has added an appropriate line of his own to set off the scene.

Mrs Ivy Taylor with her daughter Millie outside the farm cottage in Derby Road, nearly opposite the junction with Marsh Hall Road, c. 1900. Marsh Hall itself ran down the side of this and was at right-angles to it. Roy Chadwick (1893-1947) was the designer of the Lancaster bomber and was the son of Charles and Agnes Chadwick. Agnes was the daughter of George and Mary Bradshaw of Marsh Hall which was at that time a large farm. Roy and his sister Doris spent their early years here. Roy studied at evening classes and worked for British Westinghouse. He followed a career in aviation and became Avro's chief designer in 1917. He designed the Avis two-seater biplane, the Bison spotter plane, the Avenger fighter, Avro Torpedo bomber and the Andover.

Farnworth vicarage was once an imposing building, seen here about seventy years ago, but fell into a state of disrepair and was demolished.

Seven
Hale and Hale Hall

Hale Hall was started by Gilbert Ireland following his knighthood in 1617. It was finished in 1623.

This and the following two photographs show the hall from different angles and display the variety of styles on each facing side. This shows the north and east sides.

Hale Hall from the west side.

Hale Hall from the east side.

This thatched cottage was the birthplace of the seventeenth-century giant John Middleton, the so-called 'Childe of Hale'. The house has been well preserved and is worth a visit.

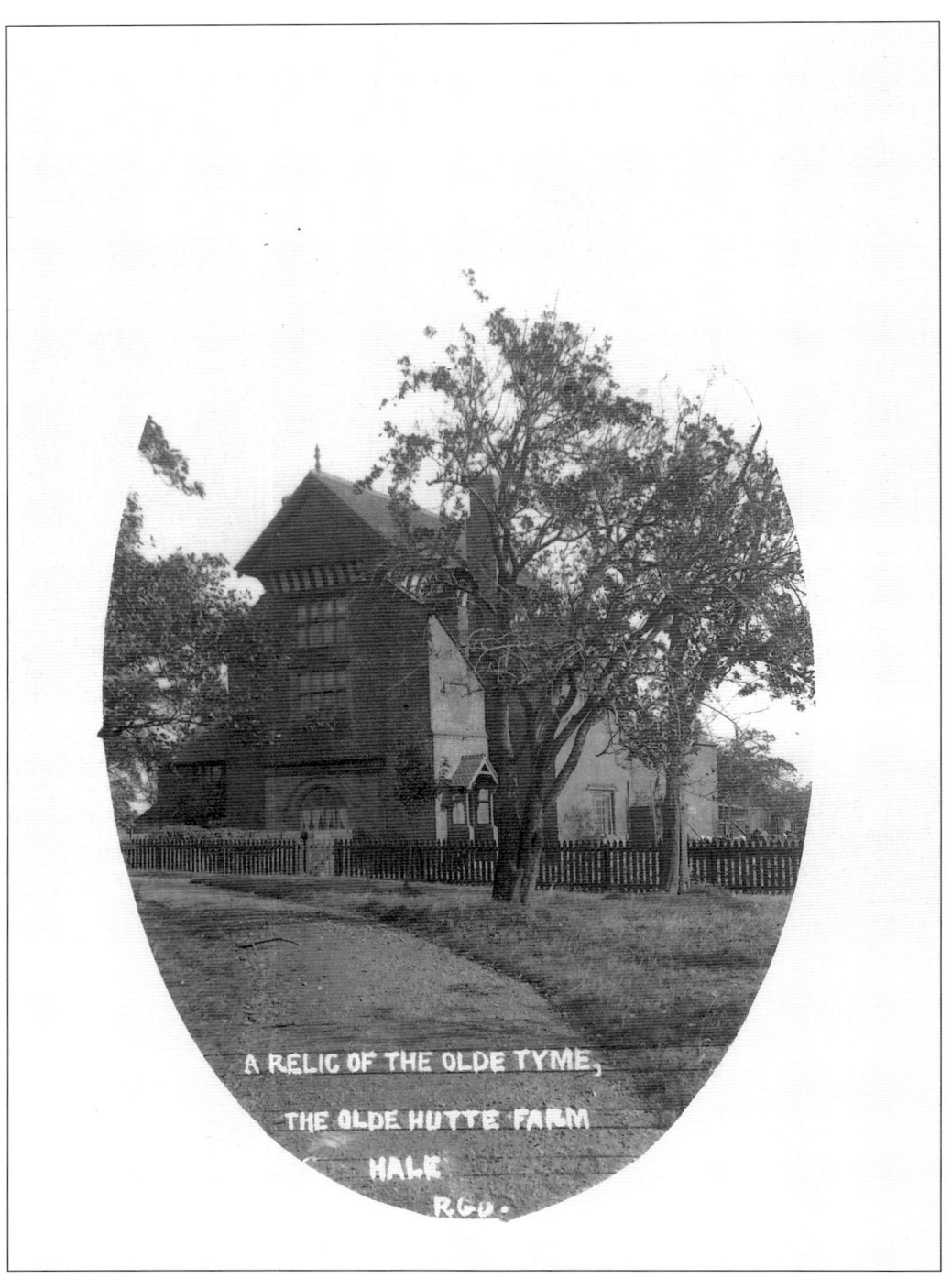

A RELIC OF THE OLDE TYME,
THE OLDE HUTTE FARM
HALE
R.G.O.

The story of Hale is a long one. Its origins go far back in time when the area was a fine wheat growing area and a place where fishing boats plied their trade from this point on the river Mersey. The Irelands were the lords of the manor and used the Old Hutte as the family home. It is thought that the family also lived in the old hall.

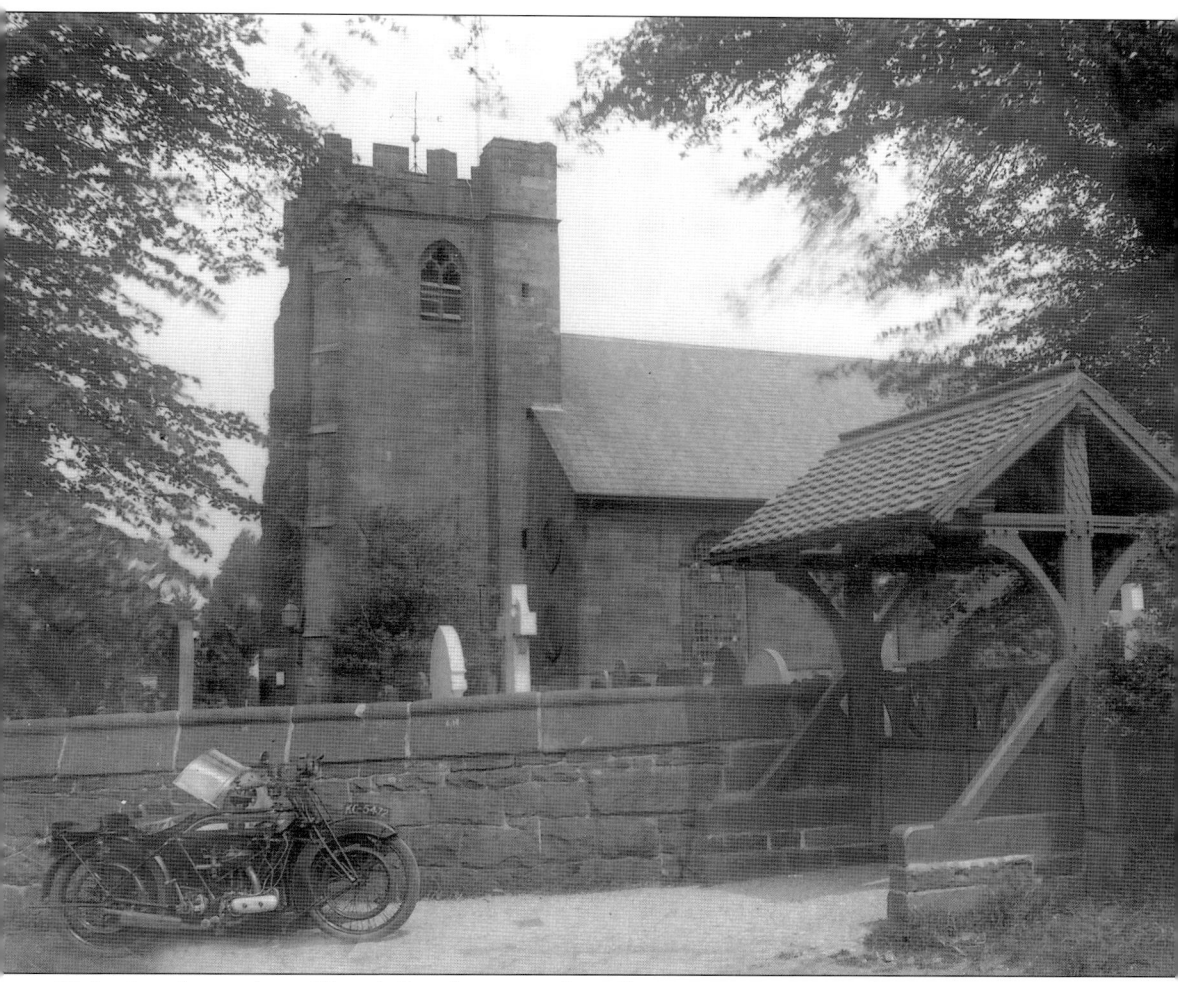

Hale church stands in Church Road near to the village centre and is on the site of a chapel erected in 1081 by John Ireland who was buried there in 1088.

A picturesque view of Hale village in the first decade of the last century.

Another early twentieth-century view of Liverpool Road In the summer flowers were sold in the village; multi-coloured dahlias and chrysanthemums.

This postcard view of Liverpool Road perhaps in the 1920s, apparently shows the post office but it is difficult to see which building it might be. Spot the little boy with a sandwich?

This is the Childe of Hale Inn, at Hale.

This is the Wellington Hotel at Hale.

The interior of the Child of Hale's birthplace. This postcard picture claims that the hooks on the roof beam were used by John Middleton to hang up his coat!

Eight
Rainhill

Kelsall's Farm in Lower House Lane, owned by landowner Bartholomew Bretherton and tenanted by Edward Kelsall.

St Ann's church, Rainhill produced as a picture postcard in a mock frame.

A group of people gather for a photograph outside the Old Ship Inn c. 1900.

Manor Farm, Rainhill. Part of the Bartholomew estate.

A view of the Ship Inn corner, around 1900.

93

The end of Stoops Lane seen entering Rainhill from the Warrington direction c. 1910.

Turning left at the Ship Inn corner we see the Avenue with its many trees c. 1900.

A postcard view from around 1900 looking across the fields to Rainhill with the asylum in the foreground.

Church Place, near to Rainhill village centre c. 1900.

The Sisters of Charity convent, Rainhill. Built on land adjacent to St Bartholomew's church, the convent still stands today.

St. Ann's church, Rainhill after it was enlarged and given a new tower and steeple, seen sometime in the late nineteenth century.

Rainhill's war memorial.

The new lych gate at St Ann's church, c. 1960.

The Towers, Rainhill was used as a hospital and recuperation centre during the Great War.

The Commandant, or matron, at the hospital during the war. The Towers is now a large private school.

Warrington Road, probably at the junction with Lawton Road, c. 1914.

Blundell's Bank from a postcard photograph by W. Hall. Photographers often visited villages to take photographs by bicycle at this time and there is one just visible on the right in this scene but it is unlikely to be Mr Hall's because apparently he used a motorbike and sidecar on his travels!

Blundell's Bank with a pair of roadworkers clearing dirt from the road in the autumn, *c.* 1910.

Cattle settle down in their Rainhill pasture, *c.* 1915.

Mount Corner another quiet place, *c.* 1915.

Mount Corner and View Road, c. 1905.

The bottom of Welsby's Sandstone Quarry, men are cleaving the layers with wedges, 1900. Some stone from here was used in the building of Liverpool's Anglican Cathedral but most of it came from Woolton. Cronton's RC church of the Holy Family was built entirely of Welsby stone.

Nine
Cronton

The Unicorn Inn and the village stocks at Cronton, c. 1910. The stocks still exist at the main cross roads. Cronton was once in the hands of the the Barons of Widnes. In the reign of Queen Elizabeth I the Manor of Cronton was in the possession of Thomas Holte and later it was acquired by a number of people, one of whom, James Lawton, died at Farnworth in 1616. Richard Wright of Cronton owned a fourth part of the Manor and on his death in 1621 it was said to be worth 30s 6d per annum. Bartholomew Bretherton bought the Wright's estate in 1821 and turned the Manor House into a delightful residence and the gardens were much improved.

Townend, Cronton, c. 1905. This, the oldest part of the village, was linked to Cronton Hall by a winding lane, two hundred yards long. Cronton Cross stood along here and was thought to have been the resting place for funeral parties. The pall-bearers would rest here whilst prayers were said. These crosses were usually on roads leading to churches, but in many places they have disappeared leaving only the name. In Widnes we have Plumpton's Cross, Simm's Cross and Cuerdley Cross as reminders of this bygone custom.

Cronton Catholic church c. 1910.

Cronton's RC church, over ninety years old, looks splendid with its Welsby sandstone and the pit, a local name for a small pond, in the foreground, here in about 1910.

Lovers' Lane End, the ideal country lane, quiet, picturesque and winding c. 1905.

Ten
People and Places

A Widnes soldier, W.B. Breeden, in France during the Great War, c. 1916. In this, and most earlier wars, men, if they had them, would take their own weapons, horses and vehicles. Sometimes vehicles were sent straight to the front from the factories, having been ordered by soldiers before they left. This soldier took his own belt drive Douglas motorcycle with him to France.

Another member of the same Widnes family, J.H. Breeden (middle of the front row), with fellow Non-Commissioned Officers during respite from the trenches in 1916.

Before and after The First World War J.H. Breeden worked on C.G. Marsh's Mount Pleasant farm near Speke. Despite the size and power of these huge horses the ploughshare has become stuck and J.H. Breeden is in the hole digging out the plough! The suspended plough will be used on the return journey and the horses will be fastened to the other end of the plough.

Two lighter horses, also at Mount Pleasant Farm, are here being used to pull a load of hay bales, c. 1916.

Most Auxiliary Fire Service teams were kept together after the war as peace time teams. Here at Washington Hall, Chorley, in 1960, the Widnes team entered the local; efficiency competition. They were, from let to right: Eric Wilkinson, John Breeden, Brian Rogerson, Dave Campbell, Ken Bibby and George Breeden.

The Widnes team did well! Here at the presentations are, left to right: Eric Wilkinson, Assistant District Officer Williams, Ken Bibby, Brenda Breeden, Brian Rogerson, George Breeden (Brenda's husband), District Officer Scott (Officer in Charge, C Division Lancashire County Fire Brigade), presenting the awards and Dave Campbell.

The new Wesley chapel at the bottom of Peel House Lane c. 1905. New kerbs and flags are being laid in the pavements opposite.

Railway cottages set in a hollow on the Bongs, seen here before 1900. The railway embankment can be seen behind the chimneys. The railway line climbed all the way to St Helens and was so steep that another engine was used to push all the way. Coming back was no problem provided you took it easy and had good brakes! The new Widnes by-pass now follows the route of this old railway and is now called Watkin's Way.

Matthew Gregson (1749-1824) was born in Liverpool, the second son of Thomas Gregson of Whalley in Lancashire. He was a blockmaker and upholsterer by trade but his business grew to take in all aspects of, what we would call today, interior design for his rich clients and he acquired a considerable fortune. The latest London designs were used and he advised clients on their furnishing needs including the purchase of prints and libraries of books. In twenty-two years he reputedly spent only three days away from his business. He bought his grandmother's old property at Black Denton, Widnes from a relation, Thomas Naylor, in 1799 and by 1809 owned the Manor and Lordship of Overton with 350 acres of land, Black Denton's farm and land inherited from his mother, as well as property in Liverpool. Several Widnes street names commemorate Gregson and his family: Black Dentons Place, Gregson Road and Naylor Road.

Mr T. Isherwood grew marvellous rhubarb in HaltonView c. 1928.

Miss Crawford speaking to the Widnes Historical Society in its early years, c. 1951. She was the first life member of the society.

Historical Society trips have been a feature for many years but full details of this 1950s visit are now sadly lost.

117

A staff outing to Blackpool from J.W. Towers, the glass manufacturers, in the late 1960s.

Miss Card poses at the gate of One Barn Farm in Warrington Road, Hatton View in the late 1920s.

Mr and Mrs Sparkes were the last known occupants of Black Dentons farm but whether they were owners or tenants is not known. Mr Sparkes displays his gardening medals and cups, *c.* 1935.

This photograph appeared in the paper 28 February 1908 with these headlines and this report, 'Widnes in a Whirlwind', 'The Effects of the Storm', 'Extensive Damage'. 'The violent south westerly gale which swept over the country on Saturday was felt with all its force, chimney pots, ridge tiles and bricks were whirled in all directions, the effect was being heightened by driving rain. Victoria Square received the full force of the gale. Ten of the Co-operative Society's large windows were blown in, the glass breaking the large mirrors in the background. Latest creations in ladies' hats, blouses, every kind of drapery was carried by the wind into the street, in some instances high aloft and in others careening along the roadway. Costume dummies bounced along the street. The Grapes public house suffered severely.'

The General Post Office at the end of the Central Stores block, at the beginning of the 1900s.

A gathering at the cottages in Moorfield Road, opposite to the Peter Spence entrance, c. 1910. Everyone seems to be in their Sunday Best – were they celebrating something?.

Looking down Mill Lane in the direction of Bold, c. 1910. At the far right can be seen the site of the old mill. The pond is still there, now by Rivendell Nursery. Knowles' farm is there too, along with a barn and stable.

A Black 5, one of many built by the LMS and BR between 1934 and 1951, seen here on the Widnes West Deviation in the 1960s.

British Rail Standard 2MT 2-6-0 No.78035 crossing the St Helen's Canal Swing Bridge from Spike Island which can be seen in the background c. 1960. There are floodlights mounted on the poles.

Locomotive 9F 92051 seen from Widnes No. 1 Signal (Vine Yard). The locomotive is returning to Sutton Oak Sheds after bringing a load of pyrites from Long Meg in Cumbria to U.S.A.C. for the production of sulphuric acid, in the late 1950s.

The cobbled lower end of Farnworth Street. The buildings on the left hand side have now gone but some shops remain on the right c. 1920.

Victoria Park in the late 1930s showing the newly paved walk leading to the lake. The lake had problems. Its lining cracked and the water drained away so it was converted into a rose garden.

A view of Halton Castle from Widnes Marsh from a painting by George Williams made into a colour postcard in the early years of the twentieth century.

A crowd awaits the arrival of Queen Elizabeth the Queen Mother at the junction of Farnworth Street and Derby Road 6 May 1958. The Griffin Hotel has some good stained glass windows depicting scenes in the Bold area.

And here she is! The Queen Mother about to leave the Transporter bridge and begin her tour of the town, with a ready smile for everyone.

Phyllis and Florence, the Davies twins, in their Sunday best in the early 1900s. Florence married a Breeden and was mother to George.